# contents

# Introduction

When she was seventeen, Karen's family was on vacation in the south of France. Karen saw an ad for a modeling contest in a newspaper. She went to the contest and she won.

When Shalom was sixteen, she went to a show by The Cure in Toronto. An agent saw her and said, "Do you want to be a model?"

Supermodels Karen Mulder and Shalom Harlow started their modeling lives in this way. Every supermodel has a story about the beginning. They all remember this important time in their lives.

After that, life changes. Supermodels are rich and famous. Everybody knows their faces. Everybody knows that their lives are wonderful. Big money, different countries, beautiful clothes, wonderful parties . . . !

But is the life of a supermodel all easy? The models get big money. But they say that they work very hard for it. What do you think? In this book, you will learn about the lives of today's supermodels.

Vicky Shipton is from Michigan, in the United States. She lived in Turkey and Britain for a long time. Now she is in America again. She lives in Madison, Wisconsin, with her husband and two daughters.

Vicky wrote this book because she is interested in the world of fashion. She studied fashion when she was younger. But she doesn't want to work in fashion now!

# TAKE THE
# SUPERMODEL
## TEST

Do you want to be a supermodel? Answer these questions with YES or NO.

**1**    **Are you tall (over 1.72 meters)?**

**2**    **Do friends say that you are beautiful or pretty?**

**3**    **Are your teeth good?**

**4**    **Do people look at you when you walk into a room?**

**5**    **Do you like it when they look at you?**

**6**    **Do you do a lot of exercise?**

**7**    **Do you have a good body?**

**8**    **Do you work hard?**

**9**    **Do you love clothes?**

**10**  **Do you WANT to be a model?**

Did you answer YES to eight or more of these questions? Maybe you *can* be a supermodel. But remember . . . many people want to be supermodels. But not many people *become* supermodels.

# PEOPLE IN THE FASHION WORLD

**DESIGNERS** Fashion designers have ideas for new clothes. Calvin Klein and Vera Wang are famous designers.

**MODELS** Models wear the designers' new clothes in runway shows and in magazines. When does a model become a **supermodel**? It's a difficult question. Only the richest and most famous models are "supermodels."

**PHOTOGRAPHERS** Photographers take pictures for magazines. A picture on the cover of a magazine is very important!

**CLIENTS** Models sell things for clients. Clients are magazines, clothes designers, or companies. A model in a perfume ad is selling the company's perfume with her face.

**AGENTS** Agents put the right model with the right client for a job. The agent usually gets about 20% of the model's money. They take 20% of the client's money, too. Most models are with an **agency**.

# Do You Know
## Your Supermodels?

**Try these questions! How much do you know about the supermodels of today?**

**1** **Which supermodel was Richard Gere's wife?**
a Elle Macpherson  b Cindy Crawford  c Claudia Schiffer

**2** **Most of the agencies in her home town said "no" to one model. Which model?**
a Linda Evangelista  b Christy Turlington  c Tyra Banks

**3** **Which supermodel doesn't like to look at her pictures?**
a Christy Turlington  b Shalom Harlow  c Cindy Crawford

**4** **Which supermodel did _not_ work for MTV?**
a Cindy Crawford  b Stephanie Seymour  c Amber Valletta

**5** **Which supermodel was with singer Axl Rose?**
a Tyra Banks  b Amber Valletta  c Stephanie Seymour

**6** **Which supermodel is "The Body" in her home country?**
a Kate Moss  b Claudia Schiffer  c Elle Macpherson

**7** **Which supermodel says that she will not do runway shows now?**
a Claudia Schiffer  b Christy Turlington  c Shalom Harlow

**8** **Actor Johnny Depp gave a BMW to a supermodel. Which model?**
a Kate Moss  b Linda Evangelista  c Amber Valletta

**9** **The first supermodel doll was in the stores in 1995. Who was it?**
a Cindy Crawford  b Kate Moss  c Karen Mulder

**10** **Which supermodel changed her hair color seventeen times in two years?**
a Linda Evangelista  b Amber Valletta  c Shalom Harlow

See page 29 for the answers.

# The First
# Supermodels

**Somebody first used the word "supermodel" in the 1980s. But there were supermodels a long time before that.**

**John Robert Powers, an actor, started the first modeling agency in New York in 1923. He started the agency after he got thirty dollars for a photo. His first models were other actors.**

**Years later, the modeling world was very different. In the 1960s, top models were as famous as movie actors.**

### JEAN SHRIMPTON

British model Jean Shrimpton was one of the faces of the 1960s. Her photos were new and exciting. She had a contract with Yardley. She married her photographer.

### TWIGGY

Lesley Hornby—"Twiggy"—was born in England. In the 1960s, she was the youngest supermodel. Some people say that she was "the Kate Moss of the 1960s." The name Twiggy means "very thin!"

## VERUSCHKA

German model Veruschka, or Vera, was a supermodel in the 1960s. She was on the cover of Vogue magazine thirteen times.

## LAUREN HUTTON

In the 1970s, American model Lauren had a $250,000 contract with Revlon. This was the first modeling contract for big money.

## CHRISTIE BRINKLEY

People called Christie Brinkley the "all-American girl." She was most famous in the 1980s. She married singer Billy Joel, but it ended.

## IMAN

Iman was the first African supermodel. She was born in Somalia. She opened the door for other black models. Her husband is the singer David Bowie.

# Naomi CAMPBELL

## Know Your Supermodels

| | |
|---|---|
| **Born:** | May 22, 1970, in Streatham, London |
| **Hair:** | Brown |
| **Height:** | 1.76 meters |
| **Eyes:** | Brown, but she changes them to blue and green |
| **Famous for:** | Sometimes difficult |

Some people in the fashion world say that Naomi is difficult. Sometimes designers and photographers have to wait a long time for her. She also likes to be the first model—and the last!—out on the runway. But one designer also says that Naomi is a very good person.

## The Beginning

Naomi studied dance at high school in London. A modeling agent saw her in a park next to her school. She was only fifteen.

Naomi became very famous in Europe after she was on the cover of the British *Elle* magazine. She worked with many designers, but she always loved working with Gianni Versace. When somebody killed him in Miami in 1997, she was very sad.

Naomi enjoys many other things.
- She wrote a book, *Swan*, and she makes movies. After she was in a Michael Jackson video, she tried singing.

- Naomi's love life is as famous as her work. She was with actor Robert DeNiro, and then Adam Clayton from U2.
- Naomi does a lot of work for children in South Africa. Nelson Mandela asked for her help there.

## Up and Down

Supermodels have accidents too! In one fashion show in London, Naomi fell down. Her shoes were by designer Vivienne Westwood and they were very high!

"I don't have to ask. They give it to me."
Naomi Campbell

# Amber **VALLETTA**

## Know Your Supermodels

**Born:**　　　February 9, 1975, in Tulsa, Oklahoma
**Hair:**　　　 Brown
**Height:**　　 1.75 meters
**Eyes:**　　　 Green
**Famous for:** A nice person!

A modeling agency in Tulsa found Amber Valletta, but she didn't stay in the United States. She left for Milan. Amber became very famous in Europe. All of the photographers and magazines wanted to work with her.

Amber is the best friend of supermodel Shalom Harlow. The two models were young when they worked in Paris. Then, they lived in the same apartment in New York City.

## Did You Know?

- Amber likes candy.
- She smokes.
- She doesn't eat meat.
- She is in a movie with Harrison Ford—*What Lies Beneath*.

Amber is on the cover of more than 100 magazines. She worked with Versace, Calvin Klein, and many other famous designers. In 1996, she became the new face for Elizabeth Arden. She sells the company's perfume.

When she was very young, Amber saw a film in school about a hospital. Years later, when she was famous, she got a lot of money for the hospital. She visited sick children there. Amber also helps people with no money in her home town.

"Now I can put on something and feel pretty."
Amber Valletta

# Claudia **SCHIFFER**

## Know Your Supermodels

**Born:**        August 25, 1970, in Düsseldorf, Germany
**Hair:**        Blonde
**Height:**      1.8 meters
**Eyes:**        Blue
**Famous for:** A great smile

## The Beginning

Two people from the Paris modeling agency Metropolitan saw Claudia Schiffer at a dance in Düsseldorf. She was seventeen.

Claudia had a bad start in her work. There was a problem at her first runway show in 1990. She fell down on the runway. Claudia now says that she won't do runway shows. But she has a lot of other modeling work. She had a four-year contract with Revlon. She made $6,000,000 for thirty days' work each year.

Claudia Schiffer has more magazine covers than other supermodels—400. But Claudia gets bored very easily. She likes to do different things in her work. For two years she wasn't on the cover of any fashion magazines. She was only on other magazines.

After she took off her clothes for a car ad, she became *more* famous. She also took off her clothes with Sylvester Stallone in an ad for Gianni Versace.

Claudia was with David Copperfield, but they separated after six years. Now, she is going to marry Tim Jeffries. He was with Elle Macpherson before Claudia!

"Claudia doesn't like to do the same thing."
Claudia Schiffer's agent, Arline Souliers

# "I Want to be a Model!" 1

SARAH AND KAREN ARE BEST FRIENDS.

Look at her clothes and hair. I want to be a model. Do you?

I don't know.

I do. I want to be famous.

SUDDENLY . . .

Listen!

I have to go! Will you come, too, Karen . . . PLEASE?

The New Face modeling agency is looking for new models. They will be here in town on Saturday morning at . . .

Oh . . . OK.

More on page 20 . . .

13

# Kate **MOSS**

## Know Your Supermodels

**Born:** January 16, 1974, in Croydon, England
**Hair:** Brown
**Height:** 1.69 meters
**Eyes:** Brown
**Famous for:** Very thin

When Kate Moss was fourteen, her family went to the Bahamas for a vacation. On the way home modeling agent Sarah Doukas saw Kate on the airplane. So Kate went to Sarah's agency. "I felt very small in this big place," Kate said.

Then, in the early 1990s, Kate worked with the photographer Corinne Day on some photos, "Summer of Love." The photos became very famous. They showed the world of London at that time. After that, Kate often worked with Corinne Day.

Kate did many ads for Calvin Klein clothes. She got $4,000,000 for 100 days of work. Kate also did ads for Yves Saint Laurent's perfume, Opium.

## Love Life

Kate was with actor Johnny Depp for about four years. But they separated when Depp became a father. The baby's mother was an actor in one of his movies.

Kate Moss wasn't always happy. At the start of her modeling life, she was sick. She was always tired and she couldn't get out of bed. In 1998, Kate was sick again. She stayed in a small hospital in London for a month. It cost $500 for each day. When she left the hospital, she found a new BMW at her house. It was from her old boyfriend, Johnny Depp. She went out for a drive. When she was out, a fire started in her apartment.

"One day I said, 'I can't do this . . .' I was not very happy."
Kate Moss

# Cindy **CRAWFORD**

## Know Your Supermodels

**Born:** February 20, 1966, in De Kalb, Illinois
**Hair:** Brown
**Height:** 1.75 meters
**Eyes:** Brown
**Famous for:** A smart model

Cindy was a smart student. After high school, she went to college in Chicago. She got 100% on one test there.

After she started modeling, Cindy was in *Playboy* magazine with no clothes. The photos changed the idea of supermodels. Before that time, supermodels didn't usually take off their clothes for photos.

## Love Life

Cindy married movie actor Richard Gere. Newspapers and magazines wanted to know everything about their lives, and they wrote a lot of stories about them. In May 1994, Cindy and Richard paid for an ad in a British newspaper because they wanted to stop the stories. They separated a short time after that. Then Cindy married Rande Gerber. He has many restaurants. They had a son in 1999.

Cindy is very smart about her work. She has a company and is always busy.

- She has calendars and exercise videos.
- She was on a fashion show on MTV.
- She does ads for Revlon. All of her ads are for big companies. She did an ad for Pepsi, too.
- She was in a 1995 movie, *Fair Game*, with William Baldwin.

Cindy Crawford—a smart model.

# Shalom **HARLOW**

## Know Your Supermodels

**Born:** December 5, 1974, in Oshawa, Canada
**Hair:** Brown
**Height:** 1.80 meters
**Eyes:** Blue
**Famous for:** Her runway walk

Shalom's first year in Paris was 1992. She modeled in every runway show there. Some people say that Shalom has the best runway walk. Maybe she walks well because she studied dance.

## The Beginning

When Shalom was sixteen, she went to a show by The Cure in Toronto. An agent saw her and said, "Do you want to be a model?"

Shalom and Amber Valletta were new models in Paris at the same time. They were good friends. Karl Lagerfeld liked using the two models in shows. He calls them "the Laurel and Hardy of fashion!"

Shalom was in the Pirelli calendar and she worked for the designer Donna Karan. For an ad, she gets $25,000 or more. For a runway show, she gets $12,000 or more.

## Did You Know?

- Shalom doesn't eat meat.
- She is in some movies. She was also on the television show *House of Style* on MTV. She left after one year.

Shalom has the best runway walk.

# "I Want to be a Model!" 2

More on page 38 . . .

# Niki TAYLOR

## Know Your Supermodels

**Born:**     March 5, 1976, in Fort Lauderdale, Florida

**Hair:**     Blonde

**Height:**     1.80 meters

**Eyes:**     Green/brown

**Famous for:** "All-American" look

## The Beginning

When she was thirteen years old, Niki Taylor saw model Christie Brinkley. From that time, Niki was interested in modeling. Her mother sent photos of her to agencies in Florida. Then, Niki won a contest in New York.

Niki started modeling for magazines. She became more and more famous. She also became rich. When she was sixteen, she had $1,000,000! Niki was the youngest model on the cover of *Vogue* magazine. When she was only seventeen, she got a contract with L'Oréal for over $1,000,000. Niki does a lot of magazine covers and she works for Cover Girl and Pepsi.

## $ $ $ $ $

- For one day's work, Niki can get $15,000!
- In one year, she makes about $4,000,000!

Niki's sister Krissy was a model, too. She worked very hard and she became sick. She died in 1995, when she was only seventeen. Niki was nineteen at the time.

Modeling isn't everything for Niki Taylor. Her two sons, Jake and Hunter, are the most important things in her life.

To Niki Taylor, one of life's most important lessons is: "Catch it before it falls."

Niki Taylor is the "all-American" supermodel.

# Linda **EVANGELISTA**

## Know Your Supermodels

**Born:** May 10, 1965, in St. Catharines, Ontario, Canada
**Hair:** Brown (but it changes all the time)
**Height:** 1.76 meters
**Eyes:** Blue/green
**Famous for:** Short hair

Linda Evangelista is Canadian. When she was fourteen, she was in the Miss Niagara beauty contest. She didn't win, but somebody from the Elite modeling agency saw her there. She became a model with Elite when she was eighteen.

Linda became a supermodel after she cut her hair in 1989. The short hair was the idea of photographer Peter Lindbergh. Now Linda is famous for it. She also loves to change the color of her hair. In four years she changed it seventeen times!

## Stay in bed!

Many people became angry when Linda spoke about modeling and money. What did she say? "I won't get out of bed for under $10,000."

Linda is one of the busiest supermodels:
- In 1999 she was on the covers of German and British *Vogue* in the same month.

- She worked for Clairol. (They make hair colors!)
  She did many runway shows.
- She was also in two videos by singer George Michael.

## Love Life

- Linda married a modeling agent when she was young. He was an older man. They separated after six years.
- She was with actor Kyle MacLachlan for many years, but they didn't marry.
- In July 1999, she married a Frenchman, Fabien Barthez. She is not with him now.

Linda Evangelista is famous for her short hair.

# Tyra **BANKS**

## Know Your Supermodels

**Born:**     December 4, 1973, in Los Angeles,
              California
**Hair:**     Brown
**Height:**   1.75 meters
**Eyes:**     Brown
**Famous for:** Great runway walk

When Tyra Banks was young, she went to an expensive school.
She had to wear school clothes there. Outside school, Tyra
wanted to look different. She bought old clothes and she made
clothes with her mother. Sometimes, students could wear other
clothes at Tyra's school. Tyra always looked wonderful on those
days.

Tyra was interested in modeling because one of her friends was a
model. Tyra went to the modeling agencies in her town. They all
said no. Then one agency, L.A. Models, said yes. But the
modeling agent said to Tyra, "I don't think that the camera likes
your face." So Tyra only modeled on the runway for her first year.

In her first year in Paris, she modeled in twenty-five fashion shows.
She worked with Chanel, Christian Dior, and Yves Saint Laurent.
The camera loved Tyra then! Now she gets $30,000 for a runway
show. She is on over 100 covers too!

Tyra is important to many African-American women. She was
the first black model on the covers of *GQ*, *Sports Illustrated*, an

*Victoria's Secret*. Tyra also likes helping people. She helps the Center for Children and Families in New York City. She gives money to her old high school. Now other girls can go to Tyra's school—and wear those school clothes!

## Off the Runway

- Tyra acts in movies and television shows. Her first big movie was *Higher Learning* with Laurence Fishburne and Ice Cube.
- Tyra also wrote a book, *Tyra's Beauty, Inside and Out*.

Models are always "waiting for the next job . . ."
Tyra Banks

# A Dangerous Life?

Supermodels are always in the newspapers, but sometimes the storie aren't happy.

In 1997, Naomi Campbell fell in London. She was very sick. Her stomach hurt and she had to go to the hospital.

In 1998, Kate Moss was in a London hospital for one month becaus she was very tired. The model later spoke about her problem witl drinking and drugs.

Of course, everybody is sick sometimes, but is the life of a supermode more dangerous than ours? Supermodels' lives are fast and busy. The often don't eat much because they have to be very thin.

But why do they have to be thin? Some designers only use very thi models. Kate Moss modeled for Calvin Klein jeans in 1993. Som people didn't like those ads. They say that the model looked sick i them.

Because they want to be thin, some models become sick wit anorexia. People with anorexia have a problem with food. The usually become very thin. But they think that they are fat. They don eat much. Some people with anorexia die.

What do young girls think when they see very thin models i magazines? Is this a problem? Some people say that bigger models ar better. What do you think?

There are many other problems in the world of modeling. Some peop say that there are a lot of drugs. One model says that she started to tak drugs at fifteen. She says that somebody at the modeling agency gav them to her. Drinking is also a problem. Some models drink at fashio shows. Kate Moss says that she drank at every show for ten years.

In 1999, a BBC television show discussed another problem. The ilmed modeling agencies in Europe. The makers of the show say that nen in agencies often sleep with young models. The models are uddenly in a fast world of parties, drugs, and drinking, and sometimes hey can't say no.

Eileen Ford tried to help young models. Her agency, Ford Models, vas very good to its models.

Cindy Crawford thinks that agencies have to be good to their new upermodels. They have to look after them well. Her agency was good o her. So Cindy didn't "run away back to Illinois and never model gain."

# Answers to *Do You Know Your Supermodels?*
## (page 3)

**1 b    2 c    3 a    4 b    5 c    6 c    7 a    8 a    9 c    10 a**

**8—10**
**You know the world of fashion very well.**
**Stop reading magazines all the time!**

**5—7**
**You know a lot about supermodels.**
**Read this book and learn more!**

**0—4**
**You don't know much about supermodels.**
**Read this book carefully!**

# Christy **TURLINGTON**

## Know Your Supermodels

**Born:** January 2, 1969, in Walnut Creek, California
**Hair:** Brown
**Height:** 1.77 meters
**Eyes:** Green
**Famous for:** Beautiful face

## The Beginning

A San Francisco photographer saw Christy on her horse when she was thirteen. But Christy didn't want to model then. She waited and finished high school. When she was eighteen, she went to Ford Models.

When Christy started modeling, her friends didn't know about her work. Then, she started working for Calvin Klein. More and more jobs followed. In 1992, Christy made $1,700,000.

Christy was rich and famous, but she wanted to go to college. She studied in New York. She says that maybe she will be a writer after modeling. Christy climbed a mountain and wrote about it. She sold the story to a magazine.

Christy is now a clothes designer. She makes women's sports clothes with Puma. They are very expensive.

# Did You Know?

- Christy loves exercise. She doesn't smoke or drink.
- Christy started a restaurant—the Fashion Café—with Naomi Campbell, Elle Macpherson, and Claudia Schiffer.
- Christy doesn't like to look at her photos!

The beautiful face of Christy Turlington.

# Stephanie SEYMOUR

## Know Your Supermodels

**Born:** July 23, 1968, in San Diego, California
**Hair:** Brown
**Height:** 1.77 meters
**Eyes:** Green
**Famous for:** Photos with no clothes

Stephanie Seymour was always interested in modeling. She started when she was fourteen. She modeled for newspapers and stores in her town. Then, she was in the Elite "Look of the Year" contest. She lost, but she didn't stop. She went to New York and modeled there.

## No Clothes

In 1991, Stephanie had a young baby, but she was in *Playboy* magazine with no clothes. Stephanie says that she isn't pretty with her clothes on!

In 1993, she started her runway work. Then in 1994, she did some famous photos for Versace jeans and Egoiste. After that, she was a supermodel. Other modeling jobs followed. She now works for Versace and L'Oréal. She became a model for Victoria's Secret clothes, too!

# Love Life

- Stephanie was with the singer Axl Rose of Guns N' Roses. She was in one of the Guns N' Roses' videos. She and Axl separated in 1993.
- Then, she was with actor Warren Beatty for a short time.
- In June, 1995, she married Peter Brant. Robert DeNiro was there. Naomi Campbell, Claudia Schiffer, and Kate Moss went, too.

Stephanie has two sons—Peter and Harry—with Peter Brant. In her free time, Stephanie loves playing with her three boys.

Stephanie Seymour models Chanel.

# Elle MACPHERSON

## Know Your Supermodels

**Born**: March 29, 1964, in Sydney, Australia
**Hair:** Light brown
**Height:** 1.82 meters
**Eyes:** Brown
**Famous for:** Great body

In Australia people call Elle Macpherson, "the body." That body gave Elle a wonderful modeling start. Her photo was in every Elle magazine from 1982 to 1988. In the 1990s, there were Elle Macpherson calendars and clothes. In 1998, a magazine called her the richest supermodel in the world.

## Off the Runway

Elle enjoys acting in movies and on TV shows. She was in the 1994 movie *Sirens* with Hugh Grant and the 1997 movie *Batman and Robin* with George Clooney. She was also in the TV show *Friends* for six weeks.

Elle loves being a mom. She has a son, Flynn. She takes him with her everywhere. She lives with her boyfriend, Arpad Busson. She was with Tim Jeffries. He is now with Claudia Schiffer.

# A Bad Time

In 1997, an old boyfriend went into her house. He took some money and pictures. He asked Elle for $60,000 for the pictures. She didn't pay him. She told the police and they caught the man.

"I am at a good place in my life right now."
Elle Macpherson

# Karen **MULDER**

## Know Your Supermodels

**Born:**       June 1, 1968, in Vlarrdingen, Holland
**Hair:**        Blonde
**Height:**    1.77 meters
**Eyes:**        Blue
**Famous for:** Blonde hair

"How can I be a famous supermodel?" people ask. Karen Mulder's answer to this question is easy—"hard work." Karen works very hard.

## The Beginning

When she was seventeen, Karen's family was on vacation in the south of France. Karen saw an ad for a modeling contest in a newspaper. She went to the contest and she won.

Karen began modeling in Paris and she stayed there. After three years, she was on the cover of British *Vogue*. Then she was in ads for Tyen and Nivea. Now she works with Guess?, Calvin Klein, Ralph Lauren, Yves Saint Laurent fashion and their perfume Rive Gauche. She lives in Monaco.

Karen isn't the only model in her family. Her younger sister, Saskia, started modeling after she finished college. So, maybe there will be two famous Mulders?

# Off the Runway

- In 1995, a company made a Karen Mulder doll. Now there are dolls of many supermodels.
- People can read *Karen Mulder: Beauty* on their computers. They can also see pictures of her.

Karen Mulder is famous for her beautiful blonde hair.

# "I Want to be a Model!" 3

# Supermodels
## "SUPER-PROBLEMS"

Supermodels get big money. Sometimes they get big problems, too.

Linda Evangelista had to leave a fashion show in Portugal in 1998. Some fashion people say that she was a little fat.

One of Naomi Campbell's workers says that Naomi hit her with a telephone!

In 1999, Cindy Crawford started a TV show, Sex with Cindy Crawford. It was about men and women. Not many people liked the show.

## Fashion and Food

A restaurant, the Fashion Café, opened in 1997. Supermodels Naomi Campbell, Christy Turlington, Elle Macpherson, and Claudia Schiffer gave their names to it. There were eight restaurants around the world, but two of them closed. Some of the supermodels left, and now only

Naomi Campbell works with the restaurant. Cindy Crawford didn't give her name to the restaurant—she bought some of Planet Hollywood!

# The End of Supermodels?

Today, some people in the fashion world think that the time of supermodels is coming to an end. They say that supermodels are expensive. People look at the supermodel, but they don't look at the clothes. One designer doesn't use supermodels. "Now the clothes are important again," he says.

Now, there are many actors and singers on the covers of fashion magazines. Music companies love this because the pictures sell their singers. Fashion magazines usually don't say bad things about the person on their cover! Singer Shania Twain has a contract with Revlon.

At the same time, supermodels are doing more and more different things outside the fashion world. Most of them have calendars. Many of them want to be in movies, and some of them want to make music. A lot of supermodels make exercise videos.

Is it the end of supermodels in the fashion world? Maybe not. But many people think that it is time for some new supermodels. Who will the new faces be? Nobody knows. Is one modeling on the runway now? Is one reading this book?

# ACTIVITIES

## Pages 1-13

*Before you read*

**1**   Find these words in your dictionary. Put them in the sentences.

act     become     blonde     body     doll     exercise     fashion
height     separate

Tilly ..... a model when she was only fourteen. She has ..... hair.
She does a lot of ....., so she has a great ..... . Tilly is tall—about 1.8
meters. ..... is important to a model. She is very famous. You can
buy a ..... of her in stores! She married at eighteen. Her husband
..... in movies, but he was interested in ..... , too. They ..... two
years later.

**2**   What are these sentences in your language? Find the words in
*italics* in your dictionary.

**a**   Her photo is on the *cover* of every magazine. You see her on
the *runway* in every fashion *show*.

**b**   They are going to use my face in an *ad* for a new *perfume*. But
when is the company going to give me a *contract*?

**3**   Talk about these questions.

**a**   What do you know about supermodels?

**b**   Do you want to be a supermodel? Do the test on page 1 of
this book.

*After you read*

**4**   Supermodels say that their job is hard. Do you think this is right?
Why (not)?

## Pages 14-27

*Before you read*

**5**   Which word is it? Find the words in your dictionary.

beauty     calendar     contest

**a**   You want to win!

**b**   All models have this.

**c**   You put this on your wall.

6  Which of these supermodels do you know? Which do you like best? Why?

Kate Moss    Shalom Harlow    Niki Taylor    Linda Evangelista
Tyra Banks

*After you read*

7  What did you learn about the models in question 6? What other jobs do supermodels do?

8  Discuss the girls in the story "I want to be a model!" In what ways are they different? How do you think the story will end?

## Pages 28-41

*Before you read*

9  Find these words in your dictionary. Why do you think they are in this book?

*anorexia    drugs*

*After you read*

10  Do you think that this is the end of supermodels? Why (not)?

11  Now do you want to be a supermodel? Why (not)?

## Writing

12  Plan a page for a magazine about one supermodel. Your page can have words and pictures.

13  Write a letter to a supermodel. Ask questions about her life.

14  You write for a newspaper. Write about the good times and the problems for models.

15  You work in television. You are planning a show about the life story of a famous supermodel. Write the beginning of the show.

# BESTSELLING
## PENGUIN READERS

## AT LEVEL 2

American Life

Audrey Hepburn

Black Beauty

The Call of the Wild

A Christmas Carol

The Last of the Mohicans

Mr Bean

The Railway Children

The Secret Garden

Treasure Island

Walkabout

White Fang